Exceptional Children At Risk

Depression and Suicide:

Special Education Students At Risk

Eleanor C. Guetzloe

 Published by The Council for Exceptional Children

ELMHURST COLLEGE LIBRARY ERIC A Product of the ERIC Clearinghouse on Handicapped and Gifted Children

Library of Congress Catalog Card Number 91-58308

ISBN 0-86586-213-3

A product of the ERIC / OSEP Special Project, the ERIC Clearinghouse on Handicapped and Gifted Children

Published in 1991 by The Council for Exceptional Children, 1920 Association Drive, Reston, Virginia 22091-1589
Stock No. P356

This publication was prepared with funding from the U.S. Department of Education, Office of Special Education Programs, contract no. RI88062007. Contractors undertaking such projects under government sponsorship are encouraged to express freely their judgment in professional and technical matters. Prior to publication the manuscript was submitted for critical review and determination of professional competence. This publication has met such standards. Points of view, however, do not necessarily represent the official view or opinions of either The Council for Exceptional Children or the Department of Education.

Printed in the United States of America
10 9 8 7 6 5 4 3 2 1

Contents

Foreword, v

1. Introduction, 1
Problems of depression and suicide have been increasingly evident among North American children and youth over the past several decades. Many of the factors related to such problems are evident in exceptional children, which sometimes may go unnoticed by both parents and school professionals.

2. Synthesis of Research, 2
Research related to depression and suicide among children and youth has increased considerably in recent years, but very little information is available regarding these problems in the special education population. Most recent studies have focused on prevalence rates, risk factors, assessment techniques, contagion, and the outcomes of school programs.

3. Implications for Practitioners, 17
The primary roles of school personnel are to detect the signs of depression and suicide; notify parents; make appropriate referrals to school and community resources; to assist in follow-up after a threat, attempt, or completed suicide; and provide for continued support for a depressed or suicidal student within the school. In addition to these responsibilities, special education personnel may have others related to identification of depressed or suicidal youngsters with disabilities and the provision of appropriate individualized education programs.

4. Implications for Program Development and Administration, 26
Development of an effective program for the identification, management, education, and treatment of depressed or suicidal children and youth

requires the development of a comprehensive plan through cooperation among the home, the school, and the community. The responsibilities of the school include promulgation of a comprehensive plan for policy and procedures, training of school personnel, and provision of services within the school.

References, 35

Resources, 42

Foreword

EXCEPTIONAL CHILDREN AT RISK
CEC Mini-Library

Many of today's pressing social problems, such as poverty, homelessness, drug abuse, and child abuse, are factors that place children and youth at risk in a variety of ways. There is a growing need for special educators to understand the risk factors that students must face and, in particular, the risks confronting children and youth who have been identified as exceptional. A child may be at risk *due to* a number of quite different phenomena, such as poverty or abuse. Therefore, the child may be at risk *for* a variety of problems, such as developmental delays; debilitating physical illnesses or psychological disorders; failing or dropping out of school; being incarcerated; or generally having an unrewarding, unproductive adulthood. Compounding the difficulties that both the child and the educator face in dealing with these risk factors is the unhappy truth that a child may have more than one risk factor, thereby multiplying his or her risk and need.

The struggle within special education to address these issues was the genesis of the 1991 CEC conference "Children on the Edge." The content for the conference strands is represented by this series of publications, which were developed through the assistance of the Division of Innovation and Development of the U.S. Office of Special Education Programs (OSEP). OSEP funds the ERIC/OSEP Special Project, a research dissemination activity of The Council for Exceptional Children. As a part of its publication program, which synthesizes and translates research in special education for a variety of audiences, the ERIC/OSEP Special Project coordinated the development of this series of books and assisted in their dissemination to special education practitioners.

Each book in the series pertains to one of the conference strands. Each provides a synthesis of the literature in its area, followed by practical suggestions—derived from the literature—for program developers, administrators, and teachers. The 11 books in the series are as follows:

- *Programming for Aggressive and Violent Students* addresses issues that educators and other professionals face in contending with episodes of violence and aggression in the schools.
- *Abuse and Neglect of Exceptional Children* examines the role of the special educator in dealing with children who are abused and neglected and those with suspected abuse and neglect.
- *Special Health Care in the School* provides a broad-based definition of the population of students with special health needs and discusses their unique educational needs.
- *Homeless and in Need of Special Education* examines the plight of the fastest growing segment of the homeless population, families with children.
- *Hidden Youth: Dropouts from Special Education* addresses the difficulties of comparing and drawing meaning from dropout data prepared by different agencies and examines the characteristics of students and schools that place students at risk for leaving school prematurely.
- *Born Substance Exposed, Educationally Vulnerable* examines what is known about the long-term effects of exposure *in utero* to alcohol and other drugs, as well as the educational implications of those effects.
- *Depression and Suicide: Special Education Students at Risk* reviews the role of school personnel in detecting signs of depression and potential suicide and in taking appropriate action, as well as the role of the school in developing and implementing treatment programs for this population.
- *Language Minority Students with Disabilities* discusses the preparation needed by schools and school personnel to meet the needs of limited-English-proficient students with disabilities.
- *Alcohol and Other Drugs: Use, Abuse, and Disabilities* addresses the issues involved in working with children and adolescents who have disabling conditions and use alcohol and other drugs.
- *Rural, Exceptional, At Risk* examines the unique difficulties of delivering education services to at-risk children and youth with exceptionalities who live in rural areas.

- *Double Jeopardy: Pregnant and Parenting Youth in Special Education* addresses the plight of pregnant teenagers and teenage parents, especially those in special education, and the role of program developers and practitioners in responding to their educational needs.

Background information applicable to the conference strand on juvenile corrections can be found in another publication, *Special Education in Juvenile Corrections,* which is a part of the CEC Mini-Library *Working with Behavioral Disorders.* That publication addresses the demographics of incarcerated youth and promising practices in responding to their needs.

1. Introduction

Problems of depression and suicide have been increasingly evident among North American children and youth over the past several decades. Many of the factors related to such problems are evident in exceptional children, which sometimes may go unnoticed by both parents and school professionals.

Over the past several decades, the problems of depression and suicide have become increasingly evident among children and adolescents in both the United States and Canada. These problems are now recognized as serious threats to not only the mental and physical health of great numbers of young people, but also their very existence.

Children with physical, emotional, and cognitive disabilities are at high risk for depression and suicide. Many of the factors that have been carefully documented in research studies as being related to these problems are also evident in children with exceptionalities, which sometimes may go unnoticed by both parents and school professionals.

The following discussion will focus on recent research related to the problems of depression and suicidal behavior among children and adolescents. Some of the suggestions for school programs will be based on empirical data, while others will be based on what is considered to be the best practice in the field. Special consideration will be given to the problems of depression and suicide in the special education population and the roles of the professionals who serve children with disabilities.

The following topics will be discussed as they relate to the problems of depression and suicide in typical children and children with disabilities:

1. Recent research on depression and suicidal behavior in children and adolescents.

2. The development of school programs for prevention and intervention.

3. The roles of various school professionals in the implementation of school programs.

While this discussion focuses on the school's responsibility in providing services to children and youth at risk for depression and suicide, it should be noted that these problems are not the responsibility of the school alone. Successful prevention and treatment programs require the cooperation and support of all individuals, agencies, and institutions that come into contact with "children on the edge."

2. Synthesis of Research

Research related to depression and suicide among children and youth has increased considerably in recent years, but very little information is available regarding these problems in the special education population. Most recent studies have focused on prevalence rates, risk factors, assessment techniques, contagion, and the outcomes of school programs.

Over the last 20 years, there has been a considerable increase in research activity related to depression and suicide among children and adolescents. Areas of particular interest have been the prevalence rates; risk factors associated with suicide and depression; procedures and instruments for the assessment of depression and suicidal intent; and the contagious nature of suicidal behavior. Several recent studies have addressed the outcomes of school-based suicide prevention programs. Most of the major studies have been conducted or funded by governmental agencies such as the National Institute of Mental Health (NIMH) or the Centers for Disease Control (CDC).

There is, however, very little information regarding depression and suicide in the special education population (Guetzloe, 1988, 1989b). Very few school programs record data related to the prevalence of depression and/or suicidal behavior among students receiving special education services, the risk factors specific to this population, or the instructional procedures that may serve to alleviate these problems. Moreover, most researchers do not include information about school placements in the descriptions of their subjects. In fact, some researchers have deliberately excluded special education students from their samples (e. g., Pfeffer, Zuckerman, Plutchik, & Misruchi, 1984, as discussed later). Implications for special education programs must therefore be drawn from findings on groups of children whose disability status is not known.

Prevalence of Suicidal Behavior

Since the 1950s, there have been dramatic increases in the rates of suicide among young people in both the United States and Canada. Accidents claim by far the greatest number of lives among children and adolescents of all ages, but suicide is the second leading cause of death among young people ages 15 to 24 in Canada (Health and Welfare Canada, 1987). It is the third leading cause of death in this age group in the United States, ranking below only accidents and homicide (National Center for Health Statistics [NCHS], 1989). Suicide is also the sixth leading cause of death among children ages 5 to 14 years in the United States (NCHS, 1989). These statistics show that suicide is rare in children under the age of 15, but in the 15- to 24-year age group the rate increases with each of the teen years, reaching a peak at age 23 (Shaffer, Garland, Gould, Fisher, & Trautman, 1988).

According to the most current statistical information available (NCHS, 1989), the 1987 rate of suicide was .7 per 100,000 among youngsters aged 5 to 14 and 12.9 per 100,000 among those aged 15 to 24. Although there is limited official information regarding children under the age of 5, suicidal behavior has been reported for this population (Pfeffer, 1986; Rosenthal & Rosenthal, 1984).

The problem of youth suicide is not restricted to North America. There have also been unusual increases in the rates of suicide among the young in other countries, including Australia, Austria, Denmark, England, Finland, Israel, Japan, and Sweden.

Although the official statistics are sufficiently alarming, it is generally accepted that, because of the social stigma attached to suicide, the statistics may be inaccurate. Many suicides are misreported or under-reported. The suicides of young people, in particular, may be reported as accidental deaths or as deaths from so-called "undetermined" causes because of (a) the widely held belief that children rarely intend to kill themselves; (b) an attempt to protect the survivors from the stigma of suicide; and (c) the predominant religious beliefs of a particular country or culture (Hawton, 1986). The actual number of suicides may be two or three times greater than official statistics indicate (American Psychiatric Association, 1985).

It is generally accepted that for every completed suicide there may be as many as 100 to 200 attempts, many of which are not reported to authorities. Since 1977, over 5,000 youths have killed themselves each year in the United States alone (Moore, 1986). Based on the number of reported suicides, the number of suicide attempts by young people in the United States each year may therefore range from 500,000 to 1,000,000. These estimates of suicide attempts do not take into account that, for the reasons just noted, many suicides are not reported.

CDC Report on Youth Suicide. In November, 1986, the Centers for Disease Control (CDC) of the U. S. Department of Health and Human Services issued a surveillance report on suicide deaths among young people in the United States ages 15 to 24. The report contains an analysis of vital statistics based on death certificates and provides information on trends in youth suicide from a national perspective. The following are some of the findings reported in the CDC (1986) document:

1. Over the 30-year period from 1950 to 1980, the suicide rate increased from 4.5 to 12.3 deaths per 100,000 in the population of 15- to 24-year-olds. Between 1970 and 1980, the suicide rate in that age group increased from 8.8 to 12.3 deaths per 100,000. During that period, the rate for the remainder of the population remained stable.

2. During the 30-year period, the year that showed the highest rate of youth suicide was 1977. The rate for that year was 13.3 per 100,000.

3. The increase in the rate of suicide among young people is due primarily to an increase in the rate among young males. The rate for males ages 15 to 24 increased by 50% (from 13.5 to 20.2 per 100,000 population). The ratio of suicides committed by males to those committed by females was almost 5 to 1 in this age group by 1980. Most of the young male victims were white (89%). Suicide rates for young African-American males and those of other races also increased (20.2%), but the rates remained lower than those of young white males.

4. The rate for all young females increased by 2% during the period from 1970 to 1980. The rate for young white females increased by 9.5%, but the rate for African-American females and those of other races decreased by 34.1% and were lower in 1980 than in 1970.

5. The suicide rates for young people ages 20 to 24 (16.1 per 100,000) during the period from 1970 to 1980 were consistently higher than the rates for those ages 15 to 19 (8.5 per 100,000). During this period, however, the rate of increase was greater for the younger group.

6. The most frequent method of suicide for males ages 15 to 24 years of age was firearms and explosives (primarily firearms). The second most common method for males was hanging, strangulation, or suffocation. The primary change over the period from 1970 to 1980 was an increase in the use of firearms and a decrease in poisoning. There was also a marked increase in firearm suicides among young females, accompanied by a decrease in suicide by poisoning (primarily by drugs).

Limitations of the CDC Study. Certain limitations have been related to the use of vital statistics information in planning for suicide prevention activity (CDC, 1986). The variables reported by NCHS (which are drawn from death certificates) include age, race, sex, place of residence, place of occurrence of death, date of death, and cause of death. There is no information regarding the victim's personal or family history of suicide, mental illness, or substance abuse; physical illness or disability; family structure; socioeconomic status; or recent life changes.

There is also a time lag of 2 to 3 years resulting from the current system for collecting vital statistics data from cities, counties, and states and subsequently compiling them in a national center (CDC, 1986). This system does not support timely monitoring of trends or the swift detection of increases in rates in discrete or localized areas. States or communities that collect suicide data within their own jurisdictions may be able to detect increases in rates more quickly and initiate intervention in a more timely fashion.

Unofficial Statistical Information. Statistical information regarding suicidal behavior in children and adolescents, while not official, can be derived from the numerous studies that have been conducted on this topic. Several researchers have reported information of particular interest to educators.

Suicidal Thoughts and Attempts. According to the results of a recent Gallup Poll released through the Associated Press, one third of 1,152 American 15- to 19-year-olds have thought about suicide, 15% have seriously considered killing themselves, and 6% have actually made attempts (Peterson, 1991).

Suicide attempts lead to the hospitalization of an estimated 12,000 youngsters ages 14 and under in the United States each year (Berman, 1986; Matter & Matter, 1984). Many other attempts (as many as 7 out of 8 in this age group) do not require medical treatment and are therefore not included in this estimate (Berman, 1986). Among high school age youngsters, approximately one fourth of attempts require emergency treatment (Peterson, 1991). Hospital personnel have noted that previous unreported attempts often become known when a more serious attempt requires medical attention. The great majority of completed suicides are by individuals who have made previous attempts.

Suicidal Behavior in Young Children. Suicidal behavior has been noted in very young children (Pfeffer, 1986; Rosenthal & Rosenthal, 1984), but there is a paucity of official data regarding the rates of suicide in this population. Suicides of very young children may often be either undetected or unreported. The self-inflicted deaths of children under the age of 10 are generally classified by NCHS as accidents (unless there is conclusive evidence to the contrary) because of the prevailing belief that young children do not understand the finality of death.

Rosenthal and Rosenthal (1984) examined 16 preschoolers, ranging in age from 2 1/2 years to 5 years, who were referred to a university child psychiatry outpatient clinic after seriously injuring themselves or attempting to do so. Of these children, 13 had made multiple suicide attempts using methods that included setting themselves on fire, ingesting prescription drugs, jumping from high places, running into fast traffic, jumping into water, headbanging, and throwing themselves down stairs. When asked about the circumstances of their injuries, these children expressed a desire to die.

Suicidal Behaviors Among Typical Children and Youth. Pfeffer and colleagues (1984) studied the prevalence of suicidal behavior in children with no history of psychiatric problems. A random sample of 101 children aged 6 to 12 was selected from the school roster of 1,565 typical preadolescents in a metropolitan community of over 100,000 people. All children attending special education classes for either emotional disturbances or neurological impairments were excluded from the study.

Although the subjects had no history of psychiatric disorder, approximately 12% had suicidal tendencies. All of the children and at least one parent of each (usually the mother) were interviewed by either a child psychiatrist or a child psychologist who used a semistructured approach. The children were asked specific questions about suicide, such as, "Have you ever thought of hurting yourself? Did you ever think of committing suicide? Did you ever try to commit suicide?" (Pfeffer et al., 1984, p. 79). The suicidal ideas or actions reported by the children were similar to those expressed by young psychiatric patients in previous studies (Cohen-Sandler, Berman, & King, 1982; Pfeffer, Conte, Plutchik, & Jerrett, 1979; Pfeffer, Solomon, Mizruchi, & Weiner, 1982). Parental depression and suicidal behavior, especially among the mothers, were common in the group, and one half of the children showed signs of depression. According to Pfeffer (1986), these findings support the need for early recognition of suicidal tendencies because, until the children were interviewed for the study, they were not known to be having problems.

Risk Factors Related to Youth Suicide

Children and adolescents with emotional and behavioral disorders and other disabling conditions are at greater risk for suicidal behavior than youngsters without disabilities. A researcher at NIMH has estimated that over 90% of suicidal children and youth have associated serious psychiatric illnesses (Blumenthal, 1990), the most common of which are conduct disorder, depression or bipolar illness, abuse of drugs or alcohol, and psychosis. Depression, in particular, has been found to be a primary risk factor related to suicidal behavior in children and youth.

Recent Studies of Risk Factors. Blumenthal (1990) has identified five risk factor domains for completed suicide (as opposed to suicide attempts, threats, or ideation) in young people and has suggested that the presence and overlap of contributing factors from one or more of these domains increase the risk of suicide. The domains and contributing factors, as listed by Blumenthal, include the following:

1. Sociodemographic factors: white male, Native American, older youth, and history of suicide attempt.
2. Psychiatric diagnosis: conduct disorder, mood disorder (particularly bipolar illness), substance abuse, and psychosis.
3. Psychosocial, personality, and environmental factors: history of early loss; more stressful and negative life events; exposure to suicide; physical or sexual abuse; poor social supports; unwanted pregnancy; early marriage (particularly for females); delinquency; incarceration; running away from home; chaotic family environments; the presence of certain medical illnesses (including epilepsy and acquired immunodeficiency syndrome); and certain personality traits (aggressivity, impulsivity, cognitive rigidity, excessive perfectionism, and hopelessness).
4. Genetic/familial variables: biological relative of suicide victim (especially identical twin or first-degree relative).
5. Biological correlates: decreased serotonin level, decreased growth hormone secretion, decreased corticotropin releasing factor, and certain perinatal factors (including hypoxia at birth).

One of the most recent governmental reports on risk factors related to suicide among children and adolescents is that of a subgroup of the Secretary's Task Force on Youth Suicide of the Department of Health and Human Services. This task group listed the following as the biochemical, psychological, and social factors most closely linked to youth suicide (Davidson & Linnoila, 1991):

1. Substance abuse (both chronic and acute) in the context of the suicidal act. Substance abuse was also found to be related to the exacerbation of concurrent psychiatric disorders, which are also risk factors.
2. Specific psychiatric disorders: affective disorders (particularly depression), schizophrenia, and borderline personality disorders.
3. Parental loss and family disruption.
4. Familial characteristics including genetic traits such as predisposition to affective illness and the effects of role modeling.
5. Low concentrations of the serotonin metabolite 5-hydroxyindoleacetic acid (5 HIAA) and the dopamine metabolite homovanillic acid (HVA) in the cerebrospinal fluid.

6. Other factors including homosexuality, being a friend or family member of a suicide victim, rapid sociocultural change, previous suicidal behavior, impulsiveness, aggressiveness, media emphasis on suicide, and access to lethal weapons (especially guns).

In a recent review of research, Pfeffer (1989) listed certain variables associated with suicidal behavior in children and adolescents who were hospitalized because of their suicidal thoughts and actions. These variables included the following:

1. Depressive disorders, personality disorders, and substance abuse.
2. A sense of hopelessness.
3. Preoccupation with death (with few alternatives to death as a solution).
4. Health problems (including previous hospital admissions for medical and surgical treatment).
5. Problems with family and friends.
6. Parental depression, suicidal behavior, and violence.
7. Prevalent and frequent suicidal behavior.

Repetition of suicidal behavior after a hospital stay has been found to be associated with (a) not living at home; (b) the severity of the initial suicidal behavior; (c) age and gender (with repetition more prevalent among the older males and younger females); (d) stress and loss; and (e) social agency contact (Cohen-Sandler et al., 1982; Hawton, Cole, O'Grady, & Osborn, 1982; Hawton, O'Grady, Osborn, & Cole, 1982; Pfeffer, 1989).

Race, Social Status, and Ethnicity as Risk Factors for Suicidal Behavior. Pfeffer and her associates (Pfeffer & Plutchik, 1982; Pfeffer, Plutchik, Mizruchi, & Lipkins, 1985) studied consecutive admissions to both municipal hospital psychiatric inpatient and outpatient units and similar units in a voluntary hospital setting. They found similar prevalence figures for suicidal behavior in children from different social status backgrounds and racial and ethnic groups. These researchers concluded that race, ethnicity, and social status are not major factors in determining the prevalence of suicidal behavior in children (Pfeffer, 1986). Other researchers have suggested, however, that Native American youth are at high risk for suicidal behavior (Blumenthal, 1990; Brent & Kolko, 1990).

The Continuum of Suicidal Behavior. Researchers have found that there is a continuum of suicidal behavior in young people that includes suicidal ideas, threats, attempts, and completed suicide (Pfeffer et al., 1979, 1980; Pfeffer, Solomon, Plutchik, Mizruchi, & Weiner, 1982; Pfeffer et al., 1984). Suicide threats, gestures, and ideation are therefore all generally considered to be warning signs of potential suicide.

Depression as a Risk Factor for Suicidal Behavior. A number of studies have confirmed that children and adolescents with depressive disorders are at high risk for suicidal behavior (Carlson & Cantwell, 1982; Cohen-Sandler et al., 1982; Dyer & Kreitman, 1984; Pfeffer et al., 1979, 1984; Pfeffer & Plutchick, 1982; Robbins & Alessi, 1985). Depression has also been found to be significantly more severe among suicidal children than among nonsuicidal children (Carlson & Cantwell, 1982; Pfeffer et al., 1984). The well-documented link with suicidal behavior is the most serious feature of depression in children and adolescents.

Prevalence of Depression in the General School-Aged Population. Estimates of the prevalence of depression among the general school-aged population in the United States have ranged from 1.8% (Kashani et al., 1983) to 13.9% (Pfeffer et al., 1984), with higher rates among older children and adolescents. A study of the general population on the Isle of Wight in the British Isles revealed that 13% of 10- to 11-year-old children showed a depressed mood at the time of interview (Rutter, Tizzard & Whitman, 1981). A reassessment of the same population at ages 14 to 15 revealed that over 40% reported substantial feelings of depression. Rutter and others have suggested that the higher rates of depression in adolescence may be more a function of physical, cognitive, and emotional changes related to puberty than of chronological age (Kaplan, Hong, & Weinhold, 1984; Rutter, 1986).

Although there is very little statistical information available on depression in younger children, it is now evident that even very young children can develop this disorder. Depression can be reliably diagnosed in children as young as 6 to 8 years (Puig-Antich, Blau, Marx, Greenhill, & Chambers, 1978; Zahn-Waxler et al., 1988). Researchers are also investigating the correlates of depressive symptomology in infants (e. g., maternal separation) although the parameters of this phenomenon are not yet clear (Trad, 1986).

Prevalence of Depression in the Special Education Population. Very little information is available regarding the prevalence of depression in students who receive special education services. This is, however, an area of considerable recent and current research interest (Cullinan, Schloss, & Epstein, 1987; Forness, 1988; Maag & Rutherford, 1988; Maag, Rutherford, & Parks, 1988; Mattison, Humphrey, Kales, Hernit, & Finkenbinder, 1986; Stark, 1990).

Estimates of the prevalence of depression among children and youth with learning and/or behavioral problems tend to be higher than those cited for the general population. Through interviews with children and their parents, Weinberg, Rutman, Sullivan, Penick, and Dietz (1973) found that 49% of children who were referred to an educational diagnostic clinic were depressed at the time of the interviews and an additional 10% had been depressed at a previous time. More recently, Weinberg and Rehmet (1983) reported that over half the children admitted to a school for students with specific learning disabilities had a depressive disorder. Mattison, Humphrey, Kales, Hernit, and Finkenbinder (1986) reported that 20.9 % of children and 50% of adolescents who were referred for possible placement in special education met criteria for a diagnosis of depression. Forness (1988) has estimated that 50 to 60% of the special education population may have symptoms of depression in addition to other difficulties such as learning disabilities or behavioral disorders.

Barriers to Special Education Identification of Students with Depression. For a variety of reasons, children with symptoms of depression may not be referred for special education assessment and services (Guetzloe, 1989b; Kauffman, 1989; Stark, 1990). In particular, gifted children with depression—or children who do not also exhibit symptoms of another disorder (e. g., conduct disorder or oppositional defiant disorder) and who therefore do not disturb others—may be overlooked in the school referral process.

Stark, Kendall, and Rouse (Stark, 1990) developed a "multiple gate" process, using both checklists and interviews for identifying depressed youngsters in the school. They found that fewer than 5% of the children identified through this process as having symptoms of depression had been classified by the schools as emotionally disturbed.

Coexistence of Depression with Other Emotional/Behavioral or Learning Disorders. Depression may coexist with other childhood and adolescent mental disorders such as anxiety disorders (separation anxiety, overanxious disorder, and avoidance disorder), conduct disorder, oppositional defiant disorder, psychoactive substance abuse or dependence, or phobias (American Psychiatric Association, 1987; Geller, Chestnut, Miller, Price, & Yates, 1985; Puig-Antich, 1982). Depression has also been found to be associated with a variety of other long-lasting behavioral problems such as impaired peer relationships, poor communication, high irritability, lack of warmth, and parent-child hostility (Lukens et al., 1983). Because of these relationships, authorities often suggest that a child evaluated for any type of psychiatric disorder should also be evaluated for depression and suicidal tendencies (Pfeffer,1986).

Several authorities have also observed that children with learning problems may be at high risk for both depression and suicidal behavior. Researchers have noted relationships between cognitive deficits and depression (Brumback, Staton, & Wilson, 1980) and between diminished problem-solving abilities and suicidal behavior (Levenson & Neuringer, 1971).

In a pilot study of all children under the age of 15 who had committed suicide in Los Angeles County during a 3-year period (14 youngsters), it was found that 7 (50%) had previously been diagnosed as having learning disabilities (Peck, 1985). Pfeffer (1986) has cited depression and suicidal behavior as special problems of children with learning disabilities who are excessively stressed by the demands of school.

Depression in Children with Medical Problems. Best and Stark (Stark, 1990) have noted that children with medical problems often face extreme and/or chronic stress, which places them at risk for depression. Estimates of depression among children with medical problems range from 7% in general medical patients to 23% in orthopedic patients (Kashani, Venske, & Millar, 1981). Ling, Oftedal, and Weinberg (1970) reported symptoms of depression among 40% of a sample of children who presented for medical attention for headaches, which may have been symptomatic of other physical problems. Stark (1990) has noted that some of these studies have reported only the prevalence of major depression in their estimates, so these figures may be underestimates.

Kaplan and Sadock (1990), in their *Pocket Handbook of Psychiatry*, have included a listing of medical diseases associated with depression, including endocrinopathies and metabolic disorders (e. g., diabetes and hypoglycemia), viral infections (e.g., influenza, hepatitis, and viral pneumonias), rheumatoid arthritis, cancer, central nervous system disorders, metal intoxications, and disabling diseases of all kinds. Some of the conditions listed may be temporary problems (e.g., viral infections), but some may be diagnosed as the primary disability in youngsters with health impairments.

Assessment of Depression and Suicidal Behavior

For many years, the primary method of assessing depression and/or potential suicide has been the clinical interview, but researchers now believe that a combination of methods and instruments should be used for an accurate assessment and that the clinical interview alone is insufficient. Recent research in the area of assessment of depression and suicidal risk has focused on the development and validation of checklists and protocols to be used in addition to interviews and medical tests. Biochemical and physiological correlates of depression and suicidal behavior have also been studied by researchers in the field of medicine, but most of these studies have been conducted with adults and the findings may not be applicable to children and adolescents. Reviews of recent research on biological correlates of depression and suicidal behavior have been furnished by Asberg (1991), Stanley (1991), and Meltzer and Lowy (1991).

Symptoms of Depression in Children and Adolescents. According to the third edition of the *Diagnostic and Statistical Manual* (DSM-III-R) of the American Psychiatric Association (1987), children manifest depression in a manner analogous to that of adults, with some developmentally appropriate differences and some age-specific associated features. For a diagnosis of major depressive episode, a depressed mood or the loss of interest or pleasure must be evident. At least five of the following nine symptoms must have been evident nearly every day for at least 2 weeks and must represent a change from previous functioning:

1. Depressed or irritable mood.
2. Loss of enjoyment or interest in normally pleasurable activities (apathy in young children).
3. Change in weight, appetite, or eating habits (or failure to make expected weight gains).
4. Problems with sleeping (insomnia or hypersomnia).
5. Psychomotor agitation or retardation (hyperactivity in children).
6. Loss of energy or feelings of fatigue.
7. Feelings of worthlessness or excessive or inappropriate guilt.
8. Diminished ability to attend, think, or concentrate (or indecisiveness).
9. Recurrent thoughts of death or suicide.

For a diagnosis of dysthymic disorder, symptoms of depression that are not of sufficient severity and duration to meet the criteria for major depressive disorder may have been present for a period of 1 year. There could be occasional periods of normal mood for no more than 2 months at a time.

The DSM-III-R also includes a listing of characteristic behaviors, emotions, and thoughts that are specific to certain age groups. The following are age-specific features of depressive disorders of childhood and adolescence:

1. In prepubertal children: somatic complaints, psychomotor agitation, and mood-congruent hallucinations (usually a single voice talking to the child).

2. In adolescents: school difficulties; negativistic or frankly antisocial behavior; use of alcohol or drugs; restlessness; grouchiness; aggression; sulkiness; withdrawal from social activities; refusal to cooperate in family ventures; inattention to personal appearance; increased emotionality; feelings of wanting to leave home or of not being understood or receiving approval; and sensitivity to rejection in love relationships.

Checklists and Protocols for the Assessment of Depression. The search for appropriate screening and assessment instruments has resulted in a proliferation of checklists and protocols. Matson (1989), Pfeffer (1986, 1989) and Stark (1990) have reviewed and critiqued a number of instruments that are currently used by clinicians in the diagnosis and assessment of depression, suicidal behavior, and related risk factors. These instruments can be classified as self-reports, guidelines for observations, and protocols for structured interviews (See Chapter 3 for further discussion).

The Risk Assessment Committee of the American Association of Suicidology recently conducted a national survey to determine what procedures for suicide assessment are in current use and how satisfied clinicians are with those procedures. Preliminary analysis of the findings indicates that clinicians are not satsified with existing assessment techniques and would use new ones if they were available (Eyman, Jobes, & Yufit, 1989). According to one of the researchers, "No single assessment can adequately evaluate suicide potential" (Yufit, 1991, p. 153). The Committee is proposing the development of a suicide assessment battery consisting of a focused interview, a suicide screening checklist, a coping abilities questionnaire, and a time questionnaire. A secondary suicide assessment battery currently includes the Actual-Ideal Self Q-Sort, Experiential Questionnaire, Draw-a-Person in the Rain, and the Inventory of Psycho-Social Balance. Some components of the battery have already been developed and are currently being field-tested. According to Yufit (1991), they will probably require revisions but should be available for use by 1999.

It should be clearly understood, however, that these instruments have been designed for use by clinicians who are trained in the diagnosis and assessment of mental disorders. Considerable experience in general interviewing, as well as training related to the use of the specific instrument, is a prerequisite to their use.

The Problem of Suicide Contagion

The contagious nature of suicide, particularly as it may affect children and adolescents, has been and continues to be the subject of considerable professional debate. Most of the recent research has focused on (a) the relationship between suicidal behavior in young people and media presentations of this topic and (b) the phenomenon of suicide clusters (a series of suicides that are closely related in terms of time or location).

Several studies have shown that there is a significant relationship between media coverage of suicide and temporary increases in suicide rates, particularly among teenagers (Bollen & Phillips, 1982; Gould & Shaffer, 1986; Phillips, 1974, 1979; Phillips & Carstensen, 1988). In replication studies, however, either no significant effects were found (Phillips & Paight, 1987) or the effects appeared to be significant only in certain geographical locations (Gould, Shaffer, & Kleinman, 1988). Coleman (1986, 1987), who has conducted a review of both recent and historical suicide clusters, notes that while the causes of clusters are still unknown, they appear to be related to the news media's attention to suicides.

At a recent annual conference of the American Association of Suicidology (AAS), David Phillips, who has done extensive research on the relationship between youth suicide and media presentations, provided the following synthesis of research findings, which appeared in the AAS *Newslink* (Pfeffer, 1989):

1. There is a significant increase in youth suicide after a front page news story about suicide. The effect is greatest in the location in which it was publicized and is directly related to the number of days the suicide was discussed in the news.

2. Suicide rates may increase after fictional accounts of suicide.

3. The more specific the headline, the greater the increase after the story.

4. There are similarities between the suicide victim and those who commit suicide immediately after the story.

The AAS Public Information Committee has developed guidelines for the media (and for individuals making public presentations on the topic of suicide) aimed at lessening the contagious effects of suicide reports. According to the AAS (see "Resources" for address), the following should be avoided or minimized in news reports and presentations (and particularly in headlines):

1. Specific details of the method.

2. Descriptions of suicide as unexplainable (e. g., "He had everything to live for.").

3. Romanticized versions of the reasons for the suicide (e. g., "We want to be together for all eternity").

4. Simplistic reasons for the suicide (e.g., "Boy commits suicide because he has to wear braces.").

The AAS media guidelines also suggest that reports should not make the victim seem admirable, nor should they approve of the suicide. The imitative effect may be reduced by (a) printing the story on an inside page, (b) printing below the fold, if the story must appear on the front page, (c) avoiding the word *suicide* in the headline, and (d) avoiding printing a picture of the person who committed suicide.

The Outcomes of School Suicide Prevention Programs. Since 1983, the legislatures in a number of states (including California, Connecticut, Florida, Maryland, New Jersey, New York, Rhode Island, and Wisconsin) have passed laws requiring or supporting suicide prevention activity in the schools. Lawmakers in Canadian provinces have also pushed for support for suicide prevention programs. Where there were no state or provincial guidelines, local communities and school districts established their own programs aimed at the prevention of youth suicide. Among the many local programs are those in Dayton, Ohio; Denver, Colorado; Fairfax County, Virginia; Houston, Texas; Ithaca, New York; Minneapolis, Minnesota; Salt Lake City, Utah; and Vancouver, British Columbia. According to the AAS, there are now more than 100 school suicide prevention programs in the United States, as well as a number of others in Canada. In addition to these programs, which are specifically designed for suicide prevention, there are many others that include suicide prevention information in a unit or module on mental and emotional health.

School suicide prevention programs vary considerably from district to district, but they generally provide for (a) detection of warning signs of potential suicide; (b) reporting and referral to appropriate individuals and agencies; (c) intervention by teachers, staff, or peers; and (d) instruction for students, faculty, staff, and parents. The programs may also differ considerably in terms of (a) the setting in which the material is presented; (b) the time allotted to instruction; (c) the type of material presented; (d) the expertise of the instructor; and (e) the financial and human resources available.

The reactions of teachers and other school personnel also vary to a considerable degree. Some teachers and counselors are comfortable with the topic of suicide, while others are afraid of parent disapproval, lawsuits, or the possibility of contagion.

Although there is an obvious need to evaluate school programs for both efficacy and safety, many of these programs have been initiated without an evaluation component (Jones, 1989). According to a survey by Smith, Eyman, Dyck, and Ryerson (1987), no evaluation procedures were included in 75% of peer support programs, 40% of curriculum-based programs, and 61% of crisis intervention programs in the schools.

Shaffer and associates (1990) conducted a controlled evaluation of three suicide prevention curricula delivered to 1,438 students in the 9th and 10th grades. These researchers found that attempters who were exposed to programs were (a) significantly less likely than nonattempter peers to recommend the presentation of the programs to other students and (b) significantly more likely to indicate that talking about suicide in the classroom makes students more likely to attempt suicide. The results suggest that the programs are failing to affect attempters in the desired direction and that the presentations may actually make those students most at risk for suicide more likely to make further attempts. Based on preliminary data from this study, Shaffer (1988) called for a moratorium on curricular presentations of material on suicide and recommended instead that schools should concentrate on providing individual assistance to students who are most at risk for suicide.

Summary

Recent research on suicide and depression among young people has focused on the prevalence of suicidal behavior, risk factors associated with suicide and depression, procedures and instruments for the assessment of depression and suicidal intent, the problem of contagion, and the outcomes of school programs. Some of the more recent findings were discussed in this chapter. Very little information is available regarding depression and suicide in the special education population. The results of other research specifically related to the development and implementation of school programs for children at risk for depression and/or suicide will be cited later in this book.

3. Implications for Practitioners

The primary roles of school personnel are to detect the signs of depression and suicide; notify parents; make appropriate referrals to school and community resources; assist in follow-up after a threat, attempt, or completed suicide, and provide for continued support for a depressed or suicidal student within the school. In addition to these responsibilities, special education personnel may have others related to identification of depressed or suicidal youngsters with disabilities and the provision of appropriate individualized education programs.

The primary roles of all school personnel are to detect the signs of depression and potential suicide, to make immediate referrals to the contact person within the school, to notify parents, to secure assistance from school and community resources, and to assist, as members of the support team, in followup activity after a suicide threat or attempt. The responsibilities of special education and ancillary personnel also include the completion of a comprehensive assessment of a student referred because of symptoms of depression and/or suicidal behavior.

If the student qualifies for special education services, an individualized education program (IEP) must be developed that provides for addressing the problems noted in the assessment. Special education would then assume responsibility for the implementation and evaluation of the educational program. There are certain other implications of research findings that are specifically related to working with children with disabilities who are also at risk for depression and suicidal behavior. These implications are listed and discussed below.

Authorities generally agree that the prevalence of depression and potential suicide is higher among children with exceptionalities than among the general school population. Special educators should be aware that many exceptional students—particularly those with emotional and behavioral disorders—may be depressed and potentially suicidal. Many of the risk factors associated with suicidal behavior are present in the lives of children with disabilities.

Many depressed and/or potentially suicidal youngsters are not brought to the attention of special education professionals. The current federal definition of serious emotional disturbance includes a pervasive mood of unhappiness or depression as a characteristic of this disability, but relatively few children meet the other criteria for special education services—that the condition exists to a marked degree, that it has existed over an extended period of time, and that it adversely affects educational performance. Problems that are transitory (brought on by situational crises) would not qualify a student for special education. Furthermore, although depression, with its accompanying cognitive problems, would very likely always affect educational performance, students who appear to be performing satisfactorily (on grade level or above) are rarely brought to the attention of the assessment team. A gifted child who is depressed, for example, may never be noticed or referred unless he or she is also failing in school.

Students who show signs of depression or potential suicide should be referred for special education assessment. Although many depressed and/or suicidal youngsters may not meet the criteria for special education services, the assessment process provides a means of informing and consulting with parents and other school professionals regarding the education and welfare of the child. It may also reveal health problems, learning problems, or emotional/behavioral problems that were previously undetected. The special education assessment process should not be used instead of assessment by a mental health professional, but rather as an additional resource.

Special education assessment should include assessment of depression and potential suicide. Authorities have often suggested that evaluation for suicide potential should be included in the diagnostic procedure for a child referred for any reason to a physician or psychiatrist. Assessment instruments are now readily available that are suitable for use by a school psychologist who has been trained in general interviewing techniques as well as in the use of the instruments (See Chapter 2 for additional information on assessment instruments). Pfeffer (1989) has listed the following as reliable and easily administered checklists (with interview or self-report formats) for the measurement of depression and suicidal behavior in children and adolescents:

1. Spectrum of Suicidal Behavior Scale (Pfeffer, 1986).
2. Schedule for Affective Disorders and Schizophrenia for School-Age Children (K-SADS) (Chambers et al., 1985).
3. Diagnostic Interview Schedule for Children (DISC) (Costello, Edelbrock, & Costello, 1986).
4. Schedule for Affective Disorders and Schizophrenia (SADS) (Endicott & Spitzer, 1978).
5. Children's Depression Inventory (CDI) (Kovacs, 1980).

6. Scale for Suicidal Ideation (Beck, Kovacs, & Weissman, 1979).
7. Suicide Intent Scale (Beck, Beck, & Kovacs, 1975; Beck, Weissman, Lester, & Trexler, 1976).

Laufer and Green (1987) have developed a comprehensive approach, based on research findings, specifically for the assessment and treatment of depressed and suicidal youth. The treatment program provides for both an individualized plan for assessment and prevention of suicidal behavior and an intervention plan, with multiple components, which is implemented by a coordinated team of professionals and laypersons. A variety of models, checklists, observational outlines, and clinical tests are used in the assessment, and input is sought from multiple sources including teachers, counselors, parents, psychologists, and psychiatrists. The outcome of the assessment, the Behavioral Intervention Plan (BIP), describes the actions to be taken and which member of the team will carry out each strategy. A case manager, in conjunction with the team, makes assessments at various stages of the implementation process to determine whether or not adjustments should be made.

The assessment of suicidal risk in young people consists of an evaluation of the degree to which the various risk factors and/or precipitating events are present in their lives at that specific time. The most commonly cited warning signs of potential suicide include (a) extreme changes in behavior; (b) a previous suicide attempt; (c) a suicidal threat or statement; and (d) signs of depression. Particularly important is the act of making final arrangements or "getting the house in order" (Guetzloe, 1989a) or procuring the means (e.g., buying a gun or hoarding pills). Substance abuse is also a powerful predictor of suicide in young people. Most crucial of all is the presence of a detailed, feasible, and lethal plan. School personnel should not be afraid to ask the student directly about a suicide plan, using such questions as "Are you planning to hurt yourself? Have you thought of killing yourself? How do you plan to do this? Do you have a gun (or pills)? When do you plan to do this?" Other guidelines for counseling a student who is suicidal are included in another CEC publication (Guetzloe, 1989b).

Symptoms of suicidal behavior should never be ignored. When a classroom teacher notices changes in a student that may be indicators of suicidal behavior, immediate action is crucial. Teachers and other school personnel who detect signs of depression or potential suicide in a student must immediately notify the school contact person, who will in turn notify the parents and other appropriate individuals in the school and community. The student should be kept under close supervision and *must not be left alone.*

It is important to let the student know that adults in the school are concerned about his or her welfare. Students who are depressed or suicidal may misinterpret uncertainty or failure to respond as lack of caring (Guetzloe, 1989b; McGee & Guetzloe, 1988).

Teachers, parents, and other caregivers (as well as physicians and mental health professionals) must be able to recognize the symptoms of depression in young people, as well as the warning signs of suicide, so they can make appropriate referrals for assessment and treatment. Bauer (1987) and Muse (1990) have provided brief and easily understood descriptions of the symptoms of depression as they may be exhibited in the classroom or the home. The following is an adaptation of those and other, similar descriptions:

1. Academic signs.
    a. Unexplainable decline in academic performance.
    b. Loss of interest in school subjects.
    c. Decline in the amount of effort expended.
    d. Turning in unfinished or messy work.
    e. Giving up easily when attempting schoolwork.
    f. Complaining of being too tired to finish assignments.
2. Social/behavioral signs.
    a. Disruptive behavior.
    b. Withdrawing from social contact.
    c. Antisocial behavior (lying, stealing).
    d. Unreasonable fears (phobias).
    e. Alienating peers and/or becoming unpopular.
    f. Looking tired or falling asleep.
    g. Risk-taking or restlessness.
3. Cognitive signs.
    a. Problems in concentrating.
    b. Forgetfulness.
    c. Indecisiveness.
    d. Lack of confidence.
    e. Expressing suicidal thoughts or intentions.
    f. Preoccupation with death.

4. Emotional signs.
   a. Poor self-esteem.
   b. Irritability.
   c. Excessive complaining.
   d. General mood of unhappiness (dysphoria).
   e. Feeling guilty.
5. Physical signs (which may not be noticed in school).
   a. Changes in sleep patterns (sleeping too much or too little).
   b. Sudden weight gain or loss.
   c. Change in appetite.
   d. Complaints about illness, pain, or feeling tired.
   e. Looking or acting "slowed down" (psychomotor retardation) or "speeded up" (agitation or hyperactivity).

The Individualized Education Program (IEP) of a student with symptoms of depression or suicidal behavior should include goals and objectives related to the alleviation of risk factors noted in the assessment. Symptoms of depression and suicidal behavior should, because of the associated potential for harm to the child, take precedence over a low reading or mathematics score or other problems. The specific risk factors noted in the assessment should be included and addressed in the IEP. Special education classroom curricula should include topics, units of study, and instructional programs that address the risk factors associated with depression and suicidal behavior.

It is extremely important to include appropriate family involvement as part of the school program for depressed and potentially suicidal youngsters. Family problems are important risk factors for both depression and suicidal behavior. It is extremely important that the family receive information and support from the school, including help with referrals to affordable treatment providers (public or private). The treatment plan should include provisions for family education, counseling, or therapy, generally recognized as essential to successful treatment for a depressed or suicidal youngster. If the child has been identified as having a disabling condition, family education can be included in the IEP as a related service. To whatever extent is legal and possible, the school should cooperate in the provision of support to both the child and the family.

If the placement of a depressed or suicidal child is changed for any reason, the receiving school or program should be immediately notified, so that appropriate supervision can be effected. Information about suicide attempts or threats should be relayed to a receiving facility by telephone (or other immediate means) rather through the normal school mail, and the sending agency should carefully document this report. Such information should also become part of school records, to be forwarded with other records to the next program or school the student attends.

There are generally services available in the school and community that can provide treatment and follow-up for depressed and suicidal youth. Among community resources that generally provide assessment and treatment for suicidal youth are crisis stabilization units; psychiatric hospitals; community mental health centers; private psychologists, psychiatrists, and counselors; and other health and human service agencies. Continued treatment and followup may also be effectively provided by social workers, nonmedical therapists, mental health workers, and volunteers who have received appropriate training. School personnel should serve as members of the support team.

The major responsibilities of the classroom teacher (in either the regular classroom or the special education program) are detection and referral—being alert to signs of depression or potential suicide and reporting such behavior to the building crisis team or other appropriate individuals within the school. The appropriate procedures to follow should be outlined in the school intervention plan. In a crisis situation, it is also important for a teacher to (a) listen carefully to a student in distress; (b) take the problem seriously; (c) verbalize caring and concern; and (d) act without hesitation to get help for the student. Teachers may also be called upon (in either an emergency situation or as part of an established instructional program) to conduct classroom discussions about suicide prevention.

Discussions with students should stress (a) the resources (individuals and agencies) that are available to help students in distress; and (b) the steps they can take in seeking help for themselves, their friends, and their families in case of an emergency. Students should be encouraged to use adults within the school (counselors, administrators, teachers, and other members of the faculty and staff) as resources in getting assistance for themselves or others. They should also know how to summon help in an emergency situation when they are not in school. For example, the following are instructions for reporting any emergency situation to the police operator, as outlined by law enforcement agencies, which could be practiced in the classroom:

1. Remain calm.
2. Be patient. Allow the operator time to write down the necessary information.

3. Talk slowly and clearly.
4. State your name, address, and telephone number.
5. Describe the incident or situation as concisely as possible and give the location. If necessary, use directions such as "North," "South," "East," or "West." Do not use "up," "down," "left," or "right."
6. Answer the operator's questions clearly and concisely.
7. Stay on the line until the operator tells you that all the necessary information is complete.

Whether or not to include suicide information as part of the school curriculum is still a topic of considerable professional debate. Shaffer (1988) has suggested that classroom discussion should focus on the availability of crisis hotlines and suicide prevention agencies in the community rather than on suicide awareness. Because of the possibility of contagion related to media presentations, the use of films is not recommended (Guetzloe, 1989b).

It is extremely important that any information made available to students be simple and factual. Many school districts now require units or components on suicide prevention as part of an existing course in health education or life management skills. According to several researchers, so-called "suicide prevention" programs may do little to change students attitudes about suicide, and some may even have a negative effect on those who are most in need of help.

The question of whether or not classroom discussion can trigger suicidal thoughts and actions is still unresolved. One authority (Shaffer, 1988) has even called for a moratorium on curricular presentations related to suicide. The emphasis in classroom discussion, therefore, should generally be on solving problems rather than dwelling on them, on emotional health rather than mental illness, and on living rather than dying (Guetzloe, 1989b). However, it is very important that youngsters understand their own importance in preventing suicide—that they must report suicidal thoughts, threats, or actions (their own or their friends') to their parents or to adults in the school.

The primary roles of the special education teacher are (a) to provide a safe, structured, and positive classroom environment and (b) to provide an appropriate, effective educational program. Authorities have noted that some forms of traditional therapy may be too stressful for depressed or suicidal youngsters and may actually be dangerous. Management procedures that create additional stress or loss may also be harmful. Classroom behavior management systems should emphasize support, encouragement, gains, and rewards (rather than punishment).

Certain disabling conditions may have implications for both curriculum and treatment approaches. Individual or group therapy might be difficult for children with hearing impairments or language disorders. Children with cognitive deficits may need a more directive approach rather than traditional therapy. Students with learning disabilities may require a remedial program that addresses academic deficits as well as treatment for emotional problems. Treatment for suicidal behavior, as well as the educational program, must be tailored to each child's needs and abilities.

Students with emotional/behavioral disorders, who are at considerable risk for suicidal behavior, may require a great deal of attention from the special educator, both in and out of the classroom. The special educator, who is usually a source of considerable support for children with emotional and behavioral disorders, may be called upon by a student or the student's family to provide information or assistance during a crisis. As noted previously, this is not an appropriate role expectation for a classroom teacher or any other member of the faculty, but such a situation may arise. McGee and Guetzloe (1988) have reported on the activities of a high school resource teacher in providing continuous support, night and day, to students with emotional and behavioral disorders who were also suicidal. The interventions were "successful," in that none of the students completed suicide during the period of time covered in the case studies, but several students made attempts and threats. It should be clearly understood that a suicidal student is in danger 24 hours a day, not just during school hours. Working with these students is an extremely demanding task. Teachers who work with such students need (a) training in crisis counseling (such as that received by crisis hotline volunteers), (b) knowledge and understanding regarding personal liability, and (c) professional liability insurance such as that made available to members of The Council for Exceptional Children.

The role of the school psychologist may be expanded to include responsibilities related to crisis intervention, assessment of depression and potential suicide, and treatment within the school. Poland (1989) has suggested that school psychologists have greater responsibility than other school personnel in working with suicidal youth. He recommends that job descriptions of school psychologists and other mental health professionals assigned to the schools should include their responsibilities for working with suicidal youngsters, so that their professional insurance would cover their liability associated with this involvement. This provision might also be considered for counselors and special educators who work closely with such students.

Stark (1990), in a discussion of school-based intervention with depressed youngsters, has suggested an expanded role for the school psychologist that would include (a) training of school personnel and parents in the symptoms of depression and the need for referral, (b) using a "multiple-gate" assessment procedure, and (c) providing assessment-guided intervention within the school. Stark has also provided detailed descriptions of affective and cognitive approaches that can be implemented by a school psychologist as part of the school program.

The role of the school counselor should include the maintenance of communication between and among parents, teachers, treatment providers, and the depressed or suicidal student. The school counselor is a logical choice for the role of school contact person, who will accept referrals from teachers and other school staff; notify parents regarding signs of depression or potential suicide; and communicate with parents, school personnel, and treatment providers regarding the progress of the student. The counselor is also in an ideal position to be the primary advocate for students who are depressed or suicidal, interceding with teachers to effect positive changes in schedules or assignments. The counselor may also be called upon to supervise peer counseling programs or mental health components offered by community professionals in the school.

The school, program, or district administrator has specific responsibilities related to the education and management of depressed or suicidal youngsters. The primary responsibilities of the administrator in either the regular or special education program are to facilitate the promulgation of the school plan, provide training for the faculty and staff, and supervise the implementation of approved policies and procedures. Related responsibilities include modifications of school policies and procedures so that a safe, positive, and supportive school environment is furnished for all students.

A comprehensive and effective school program will also incorporate specific provisions for primary prevention, including (a) fostering positive emotional development, (b) enhancing physical and mental health, and (c) addressing the problems of children and adolescents before the onset of suicidal behavior. Provisions should be made for teaching and enhancing the factors that provide protection from depression and suicidal behavior. According to Blumenthal (1990), certain protective factors (e.g., cognitive flexibility, hopefulness, strong social supports, removal from stressors, and receiving appropriate treatment for an associated psychiatric disorder, which is most important) help the individual maintain a barrier to suicidal behavior. School personnel can provide valuable assistance in this regard. Cognitive flexibility and hope can be taught, and removal from stressors (particularly within the school) can be facilitated. The school can be the pivotal agency to ensure that appropriate treatment is provided. School personnel can be members of the support group and can be trained to provide follow-up treatment appropriate for the school setting.

Many of the risk factors related to both depression and potential suicide can be addressed directly, safely, and effectively within the school (Guetzloe, 1989a, b). Any inclusion in the school program that helps to enhance feelings of self-worth, security, or self-control has the potential to prevent depression or suicidal behavior. Some factors related to depression and suicide have been addressed in curricula that are commercially available, such as those developed for building self-esteem, combatting alienation, or learning self-control. Other variables that are currently under investigation may have implications for school programs, such as the effects of color, phototherapy, exercise, music, and helping others. Any positive approach that is suitable for implementation within the school should be explored.

4. Implications for Program Development and Administration

Development of an effective program for the identification, management, education, and treatment of depressed or suicidal children and youth requires the development of a comprehensive plan through cooperation among the home, the school, and the community. The responsibilities of the school include promulgation of a comprehensive plan for policy and procedures, training of school personnel, and provision of services within the school.

Most of what is considered to be best practice in the field of suicide prevention is not based on the results of careful research, but rather on traditional treatment approaches and so-called "clinical hunches." There is little empirical information regarding the efficacy of the various treatment or management approaches in the prevention or reduction of depression and/or suicidal behaviors in young people.

Special educators must infer relationships between what we know about depression and potential suicide and what we know about children with exceptionalities. Many of the suggestions for the development and implementation of programs for children with special needs, as outlined in the rest of this book, are therefore extrapolations from the research on variables related to depression and/or suicidal behavior.

There are no standard guidelines for suicide prevention programs in the schools. Although school-based programs may have common components, no one school program will meet the needs of another district. The plan for any district should be promulgated by its own committee. School suicide prevention programs vary considerably from district to district, but they generally provide for the following: (a) detection of warning signs of potential suicide; (b) reporting and referral to appropriate individuals and agencies; (c) intervention by teachers, staff, or peers; (d) cooperation between and among parents, school resources, community agencies, and the student; (e) instruction for students, faculty, staff, and parents; and (f) procedures for both crisis and long-term intervention.

Schools should exercise caution in developing a plan for suicide prevention. The issue of whether or not school suicide prevention programs might trigger suicidal behavior in youngsters is still unresolved, with experts arguing on both sides of the question. Moreover, while some evaluation studies are being conducted, there are no empirical data that support the effectiveness of school suicide prevention programs. There are, in fact, very few data to support the effectiveness of any kind of suicide prevention program. Because there is still considerable controversy related to the implementation of school programs for suicide prevention, educators should proceed with caution in developing plans for intervention within the school setting (Guetzloe, 1985, 1989a, 1989b).

The first step in establishing an effective and safe school-based program is the development of a comprehensive plan. Policies and procedures should be established for the school and/or district that clearly delineate (a) the appropriate steps to follow in the event of a student's suicidal behavior and (b) the responsibilities of the various school or district personnel in carrying out the plan—what should be done, the order in which steps will be carried out, and the specific person or persons responsible for the actions.

A school plan for suicide prevention should be a team effort by all individuals, groups, and agencies that may be affected by its implementation. Because the program must reflect the needs and concerns of students, parents, faculty, staff, and the community, representatives from all of these groups should have a voice in its development. The inclusion of students and faculty is crucial. Among school personnel who should be involved are regular classroom teachers, special educators, counselors, psychologists, social workers, school nurses, school and district administrators, school board members, cafeteria workers, bus drivers, custodians, and other members of the staff. Anyone who might come in contact with a suicidal child should be invited to participate.

Representatives from the following community services, agencies, and organizations should be invited to be members of the planning committee: mental health associations, health and human services, crisis centers, medical clinics, hospitals, psychiatric facilities, counseling centers, law enforcement agencies, courts, correctional agencies, television stations, newspapers, churches and other religious groups, volunteer organizations, and survivors' groups. Depending on the size of the community, there may be more, fewer, or different organizations and agencies with an interest in the welfare of children and youth.

A comprehensive school plan will include procedures related to all three levels of prevention—for the aftermath of a suicide crisis (tertiary prevention); for dealing with suicidal attempts, threats, and ideation (secondary prevention); and for the enhancement of mental health (primary prevention). Among the specific areas to be addressed in the plan are the following (Guetzloe, 1989a, 1989b):

1. Detecting signs of student depression or suicidal intent.
2. Assessing the student's potential for suicide.
3. Crisis intervention, including emergency assistance.
4. Communicating with a student in crisis.
5. Communicating with parents or guardians.
6. Referral to school services or personnel.
7. Assisting parents with referral to community agencies.
8. Services available in the school or community.
9. Working with community agencies.
10. Working with the media.
11. Liaison with treatment providers.
12. Followup activity after a suicide attempt.
13. Procedures to follow in the event of a completed suicide.
14. Training for faculty, staff, parents, mental health workers assigned to the schools, and volunteers.
15. Changes in school policies and procedures.
16. Modifications in programs and curriculum.
17. Providing information to students.

Members of the planning committee may suggest other components that are necessary or desirable. All possible problems should be considered; no reasonable suggestion should be omitted from the plan.

Those responsible for developing prevention strategies for the school must be knowledgeable about the services and agencies currently available in both the school and community, so that the plan will reflect only strategies that are feasible. It is important for school personnel to be sure that affordable services are available in the community before including that step in the school plan. If there are no mental health agencies available within the district—a situation that is still possible in small or rural communities (Guetzloe,1989b)—securing such services would become a first priority of the planning group. If the services are present but inadequate, the group should establish priorities for the addition of agencies or personnel. Community leaders and elected or appointed government officials should be involved in developing the plan. Influential members of the community can be of great assistance in procuring additional services.

School personnel should be sure that mental health services are available to students who need them. If a client cannot afford services, it would be unethical to release that individual without being sure that he or she is receiving services from another mental health professional. If there are no affordable services available in the community, counseling for suicidal youngsters should be made available in the school until such services can be secured (see below and Chapter 3 for additional information regarding legal issues).

The full continuum of special education services is an essential component of the intervention plan. The services available for depressed or suicidal youngsters should range from counseling, special materials, and specialized instruction within the regular school program to the provision of education in both short-term and long-term residential placements. Eligibility for special education services should not denote movement to another class or facility, but rather the provision of services in the least restrictive environment. Educational management and treatment of depressed or suicidal youngsters is often ideally suited to the regular classroom setting *with assistance from special education personnel.* Special education can bring many ancillary services to bear upon the problems of depressed or suicidal youth. It is an extremely important component of a school intervention plan.

Crisis teams should be developed for both (a) the school level and (b) the district level. Crisis teams at the building, district, and community levels can be very effective in dealing with not only suicidal events but also other types of crisis situations such as homicides, riots, earthquakes, accidents, and bomb threats. Crisis intervention teams have been established in many school districts across the country, including the Minneapolis City Schools; Hillsborough County, Florida; Fairfax County, Virginia; and the Cypress-Fairbanks School District in Houston, Texas.

The composition of the crisis teams may differ from district to district, depending on the skills and availability of school and community members. The school (building) crisis team generally includes a school administrator, counselor, the student resource officer (if one is assigned to the school), the special education or child study team leader, and the school nurse.

A district-level crisis team generally should include the district administrator or a person designated by the administrator, the director of pupil personnel services (psychologists, social workers, and counselors), and the director of special education, as well as representatives from community organizations and institutions.

The plan should also provide for a community crisis team or network of professionals. The community crisis team or network should include representatives from the school district and any available mental health institutions and agencies in the community. The members of the community network can help the schools both by offering their own expertise in crisis situations and by helping the schools gain access to services in the community.

School plans should include specific procedures to follow in the event of a completed suicide, a suicide attempt, or a suicide threat. Specific suggestions for intervention and postvention procedures are available from The Council for Exceptional Children (Guetzloe, 1989b). A school plan for postvention is also available from Phi Delta Kappa (Garfinkel et al., 1988).

It is advisable to seek legal counsel regarding the promulgation of the school plan. The issue of liability is both real and troubling to school professionals. A number of lawsuits have been filed against school districts, charging the schools with responsibility for the suicides of young people whether the suicide occurred on or off the school grounds.

School plans should include procedures for documenting referrals, notifying parents, and other activities related to working with depressed or suicidal youngsters. Several lawsuits filed against school districts after the suicide of a student have cited as a basis for the complaint the failure of the schools to notify parents. It is imperative that school personnel document in writing their efforts on behalf of a depressed or suicidal youngster.

A comprehensive school plan will also include specific provisions for primary prevention, including (a) fostering positive emotional development, (b) enhancing physical and mental health, and (c) addressing the problems of children and adolescents before the onset of suicidal behavior. A number of suggestions for primary prevention in the schools have been discussed elsewhere (Guetzloe, 1989b). Preventive approaches in the school would include

(a) meeting the basic needs of food and drink, safety, belonging, and affection; (b) building and protecting self-esteem; (c) combatting alienation; (d) providing effective models and mentors; (d) avoiding punishment; and (e) establishing long-term alliances between and among students, peers, parents, the community, and the schools. Risk factors related to both depression and potential suicide can be addressed directly and effectively within the school in both procedures and curriculum (Guetzloe, 1989b).

The outcome of the intervention plan should be a written and approved policy and procedures document. A school or district policy, approved by the school board, serves as legal protection for school personnel as well as for potentially suicidal youngsters. In the few lawsuits that have been brought by parents against school districts or school personnel following the death of a student by suicide, the absence of written and approved policies and procedures (or the failure of school personnel to follow the approved policy) appears to have made the districts more vulnerable (Poland, 1989; Slenkovich, 1986). All school personnel must receive training so that they will be aware of and able to follow the approved policy and procedures.

The policy and procedures document should be reviewed on a regular basis, with changes made as necessary or desirable. In the event of a suicide, a suicide attempt, or a suicide threat, problems may be noted in the policy, procedures, or the personnel responsible for carrying out the plan. After the crisis is over, the planning committee should meet for the purpose of reviewing the procedures and making changes deemed necessary or desirable. If there is no crisis, the plan should still be reviewed on a regular basis (e.g., once a year, along with district procedures for special education services).

Responsibilities of District, School, and Program Administrators

Administrators at the school, program, or district level should make sure that the following responsibilities are met:

1. Have a plan in place that provides for prevention of depression and suicide at the primary, secondary, and tertiary levels. The plan should be developed cooperatively by the school, community, parents, and students. It should also be reviewed and updated to reflect the changing needs of students and the resources available in the school and community.

2. Provide training for teachers and other school personnel. All school personnel (including administrators, cafeteria workers, bus drivers, librarians, and custodians) should receive training in the

symptoms of depression and potential suicide and the appropriate procedures to follow as outlined in the written and approved school policy.

3. Provide positive information to students about the symptoms of depression and suicidal behavior, resources available in the school and community, and procedures for referring themselves and others to these services. Students should be impressed with the need to trust and notify responsible adults and the appropriateness of referring friends and seeking help for themselves. They also need to know that mental illness (including depression) can be alleviated and that competent individuals and agencies are available to provide assistance in the school and community.

4. Provide a system for early recognition, referral, and assessment of students in distress. The primary responsibilities of school personnel are the detection and referral of depressed and suicidal students. Teachers and students alike can be trained to recognize the signs of depression and potential suicide and to notify the school counselor, crisis team, or other appropriate individuals. All school personnel must be impressed with the importance of immediate referral to the appropriate contact person within the school.

Referral procedures should also include special education assessment of a depressed or suicidal student. Evaluation for depression or suicidal risk should be included as a standard procedure in the special education assessment of a student referred for any emotional, behavioral, or cognitive disorder.

5. Designate a contact person to maintain communication between and among teachers, students, parents, and community treatment providers. The contact person may be a counselor, school psychologist, school nurse, or another knowledgeable member of the faculty. This person should be (a) able to deal with information in a calm and professional manner, (b) knowledgeable about school and community resources, and (c) available during the day to discuss concerns related to the student's progress.

6. Provide case management for depressed and/or suicidal students to assist in referral to appropriate agencies and following up to be sure that services have been received. All too often, even when procedures and services are in place, some children will "fall between the cracks." Students with emotional and behavioral disorders, in particular, may often be served by a variety of agencies with very little coordination of services. An effective program will require communication and cooperation among all the agencies and individuals that come into contact with depressed or suicidal youth.

7. Provide special education for students who qualify for those services and counseling and psychological services for all students in need. Assistance for students at risk for depression and/or potential suicide should be readily available within the school. Risk factors noted in the assessment process can be addressed in either the IEP for a student receiving special education services or the regular school program for a student who does not qualify for special education.

8. Provide follow-up activities within the school after a suicide crisis. The risk of suicide does not end when the crisis is over. There must be sufficient and knowledgeable staff or volunteers to implement both crisis intervention and long-term attention for students in need.

9. Provide a secure school environment. Every effort should be made to guarantee safety and security for both students and faculty within the school.

10. Build and maintain links between and among the students, the school, the home, and the community. Many authorities have suggested the creation of long-term alliances among the worlds of school, home, and work as ways of combatting alienation and establishing a sense of community in young people. Parents should look upon the school as a resource. Every effort should be made to foster trust between the family and the school.

11. Implement school policies, procedures, and curriculum that enhance the students' feelings of self-control and self-esteem. Every school policy should be examined in light of its effects on the students, rather than its administrative convenience. Some school policies and procedures may be detrimental to a student's sense of self-worth, and those should be changed. Severe punishment, with its accompanying embarrassment and humiliation, must be avoided. The school should be a place where children want to be.

12. Participate in community task forces or other endeavors aimed at primary, secondary, and tertiary prevention of depression and suicide in young people. Blumenthal (1990) has listed a number of important public health interventions that may help prevent youth suicide, including the following:

   a. Restricting the availability of firearms.

   b. Increasing the education of health care professionals and the general public regarding the warning signs, causes, and treatment of mental illness, substance abuse, and suicidal behavior.

   c. Developing ways to minimize potentially adverse effects of media presentations of suicide.

   d. Integrating information about recognition of symptoms of psychiatric illness, coping strategies, stress management, and the value of mental health treatment into school health education programs.

   e. Developing community clinics for youth at risk that offer expert assessment and treatment combined with strong community links, social support, school liaison, family education, and hot-lines staffed by mental health professionals.

f. Advocating for parity in insurance benefits for outpatient and inpatient coverage of mental and substance abuse disorders.

g. Coalition building among health care professionals, policy-makers, civic leaders, and the general public to enhance support of research and prevention programs.

She has suggested that a community task force should develop a suicide response plan before tragedies occur in the community. She has also suggested that the physician should assume the critical leadership role in such endeavors, but, especially in the light of the educational and collaborative nature of these endeavors, a school administrator might be more ideally suited to the task.

References

American Psychiatric Association. (1985, March). *Facts about teen suicide*. Washington, DC: Author.

American Psychiatric Association. (1987). *Diagnostic and statistical manual of mental disorders* (3rd ed., rev.). Washington, DC: Author.

Asberg, M. A. (1991). Neurotransmitter monoamine metabolites in the cerebrospinal fluid as risk factors for suicidal behavior. In L. Davidson & M. Linnoila (Eds.), *Risk factors for youth suicide* (pp. 177–196). New York: Hemisphere.

Bauer, A. M. (1987). A teacher's introduction to childhood depression. *The Clearing House, 61*, 81–84.

Beck, A. T., Beck, R., & Kovacs, M. (1975). Classification of suicidal behaviors: I. Quantifying intent and medical lethality. *American Journal of Psychiatry, 132*, 285–287.

Beck, A. T., Kovacs, M., & Weissman, A. (1979). Assessment of suicidal intention. The Scale for Suicide Ideation. *Journal of Consulting and Clinical Psychology, 47*, 343–352.

Beck, A. T., Weissman, A., Lester, D., & Trexler, L. (1974). The measurement of pessimism: The Hopelessness Scale. *Journal of Consulting and Clinical Psychology, 42*, 861–865.

Beck, A. T., Weissman, A., Lester, D., & Trexler, L. (1976). Classification of suicidal behaviors: II. Dimensions of suicidal intent. *Archives of General Psychiatry, 33*, 835–837.

Berman, A. (1986). *Epidemiology of youth suicide*. Unpublished manuscript.

Blumenthal, S. (1990. December 26). Youth suicide: The physician's role in suicide prevention. *Journal of the American Medical Association, 264*(24), 3194–3196.

Bollen, K. A., & Phillips, D. P. (1982). Imitative suicides. *American Sociological Review, 47*, 802–809.

Brent, D. A., & Kolko, D. J. (1990). The assessment and treatment of children and adolescents at risk for suicide. In S. J. Blumenthal & D. J. Kupfer (Eds.), *Suicide over the life cycle: Risk factors, assessment and treatment of suicidal patients* (pp. 353–385). Washington, DC: American Psychiatric Press.

Brumback, R. A., Staton, R. D., & Wilson, H. (1980). Neuropsychological study of children during and after remission of endogenous depressive episodes. *Perceptual and Motor Skills, 50*, 1163–1167.

Carlson, G. A., & Cantwell, D. P. (1982). Suicidal behavior and depression in children and adolescents. *Journal of the American Academy of Child Psychiatry, 21,* 361–368.

Centers for Disease Control. (1986, November). *Youth suicide in the United States, 1970–1980.* Atlanta, GA: U. S. Department of Health and Human Services.

Chambers, W. J., Puig-Antich, J., Hirsch, M., Paez, P., Ambrosini, P. J., Tabrizi, M. A., & Davies, M. (1985). The assessment of affective disorders in children and adolescents by structured interview. *Archives of General Psychiatry, 42,* 696–702.

Cohen-Sandler, R., Berman, A. L., & King, R. A. (1982). Life stress and symptomatology: Determinants of suicidal behavior in children. *Journal of the American Academy of Child Psychiatry, 21,* 178–186.

Coleman, L. (1986, March). Teen suicide clusters and the Werther effect. *The Network News: The Runaway Suicide Prevention Network Newsletter,* pp. 1–4.

Coleman, L. (1987). *Suicide clusters.* Boston: Faber & Faber.

Costello, J., Edelbrock, C., & Costello, A. J. (1986). The validity of the NIMH Diagnostic Interview Scale for Children: A comparison between pediatric and psychiatric referrals. *Journal of Abnormal Child Psychology, 13,* 579–595.

Cullinan, D., Schloss, P., & Epstein, M. (1987). Relative prevalence and correlations of depressive characteristics among seriously emotionally disturbed and nonhandicapped students. *Behavioral Disorders, 12,* 90–98.

Davidson, L., & Linnoila, M. (Eds.). (1991). *Risk factors for youth suicide.* New York: Hemisphere.

Dyer, J. A., & Kreitman, N. (1984). Hopelessness, depression, and suicidal intent. *British Journal of Psychiatry, 144,* 127–133.

Endicott, J., & Spitzer, R. L. (1978). A diagnostic interview: The Schedule for Affective Disorders and Schizophrenia. *Archives of General Psychiatry, 26,* 57–63.

Eyman, J., Jobes, D., & Yufit, R. I. (1989). *A 1990 survey of current suicide assessment techniques.* Paper presented at the American Association of Suicidology 23rd Annual Meeting, New Orleans, LA.

Forness, S. R. (1988). School characteristics of children and adolescents with depression. In R. B. Rutherford, C. M. Nelson, & S. R. Forness (Eds.), *Bases of severe behavioral disorders of children and youth* (pp. 177–204). Boston: Little, Brown.

Garfinkel, B. D., Crosby, E., Herbert, M. R., Matus, A., Pfiefer, J. K., & Sheras, P. (1988). *Responding to adolescent suicide.* Bloomington, IN: Phi Delta Kappa.

Geller, B., Chestnut, E. C., Miller, M. D., Price, D. T., & Yates, E. (1985). Preliminary data on DSM-III associated features of major depressive disorder in children and adolescents. *American Journal of Psychiatry, 142*, 643–644.

Gould, M. S., & Shaffer, D. (1986). The impact of suicide in television movies: Evidence of imitation. *New England Journal of Medicine, 315*, 690–694.

Gould, M. S., Shaffer, D., & Kleinman, M. (1988). The impact of suicide in television movies: Replication and commentary. *Suicide and Life-Threatening Behavior, 18*(1), 90–99.

Guetzloe, E. C. (1985). *The "Catch 22" of suicide prevention: Are we going too far?* Paper presented at the Ninth Annual Conference on Severe Behavior Disorders of Children and Youth, Scottsdale, AZ.

Guetzloe, E. C. (1988). Suicide and depression: Special education's responsibility. *Teaching Exceptional Children, 20*(4), 24–28.

Guetzloe, E. C. (1989a). *Suicide and depression, the adolescent epidemic: Education's responsibility (rev. ed.)*. Orlando, FL: Advantage Consultants.

Guetzloe, E. C. (1989b). *Youth suicide: What the educator should know*. Reston, VA: The Council for Exceptional Children.

Hawton, K. (1986). *Suicide and attempted suicide among children and adolescents*. Beverly Hills, CA: Sage.

Hawton, K., & Catalan, J. (1983). *Attempted suicide: A practical guide to its nature and management*. Oxford: Oxford University Press.

Hawton, K., Cole, D., O'Grady, J., & Osborn, M. (1982). Motivational aspects of deliberate self-poisoning in adolescents. *British Journal of Psychiatry, 141*, 286–291.

Hawton, K., O'Grady, J., Osborn, M., & Cole, D. (1982). Adolescents who take overdoses: Their characteristics, problems, and contacts with helping agencies. *British Journal of Psychiatry, 140*, 118–123.

Health and Welfare Canada. (1987). *Suicide in Canada*. Ottawa: Minister of National Health and Welfare.

Jones, E. N. (1989). American Association of Suicidology presidential address. *Suicide and Life-Threatening Behavior, 19*(3), 297–304.

Kaplan, H. I., & Sadock, B. J. (1990). *Pocket handbook of clinical psychiatry*. Baltimore: Williams and Wilkins.

Kaplan, S. L., Hong, G. K., & Weinhold, C. (1984). Epidemiology of depressive symptomatology in adolescents. *Journal of the American Academy of Child Psychiatry, 23*, 91–98.

Kashani, J. H., Venske, R., & Millar, E. A. (1981). Depression in children admitted to hospital for orthopedic procedures. *British Journal of Psychiatry, 138*, 21–25.

Kashani, J. H., McGee, R. O., Clarkson, S. E., Anderson, J. C., Walton, L. A., Williams, S., Silva, P. A., Robins, A. J., Cytryn, L., & McKnew, D. H. (1983). Depression in a sample of 9 year old children. *Archives of General Psychiatry, 40*, 1217–1223.

Kauffman, J. M. (1989). *Characteristics of behavior disorders of children and youth* (4th ed.). Columbus, OH: Merrill.

Kovacs, M. (1980). Rating scales to assess depression in school-aged children. *Acta Paedopsychiatrica, 46*, 305–315.

Laufer, C. D., & Green, C. (1987). Dealing with adolescent depression and suicide: The comprehensive approach. In S. Braaten, R. B. Rutherford, Jr., & J. Maag (Eds.), *Programming for adolescents with behavioral disorders* (Vol. 3) (pp. 71–88). Tempe, AZ: Council for Children with Behavior Disorders.

Levenson, M., & Neuringer, C. (1971). Problem-solving behavior in suicidal adolescents. *Journal of Consulting and Clinical Psychology, 37*, 433–436.

Ling, W., Oftedal, G., & Weinberg, W. (1970). Depressive illness in childhood presenting as severe headaches. *American Journal of Diseases of Children, 120*, 122–124.

Lukens, E., Puig-Antich, J., Behn, J., Goetz, R., Tabrizi, M. A., & Davies, M. (1983). Reliability of the psychosocial schedule for school-age children. *Journal of the American Academy of Child Psychiatry, 22*, 29–39.

Maag, J. W., & Rutherford, R. B. (1988). Review and synthesis of three components for identifying depressed students. In R. B. Rutherford, C. M. Nelson, & S. R. Forness (Eds.), *Bases of severe behavioral disorders of children and youth* (pp. 205–230). Boston: Little, Brown.

Maag, J. W., Rutherford, R. B., & Parks, B. T. (1988). Secondary school professional's ability to identify depression in adolescents. *Adolescence, 23*(89), 73–82.

Matson, J. L. (1989). *Treating depression in children and adolescents*. New York: Pergamon.

Matter, D., & Matter, R. (1984). Suicide among elementary school children: A serious concern for counselors. *Elementary School Guidance and Counseling, 18*, 260–267.

Mattison, R. E., Humphrey, J., Kales, S., Hernit, R., & Finkenbinder, R. (1986). Psychiatric background and diagnosis of children evaluated for special class placement. *Journal of Child Psychiatry, 25*, 514–520.

McGee, K., & Guetzloe, E. (1988). Suicidal emotionally handicapped students: Tips for the classroom teacher. *Pointer, 32*(4), 7–10.

Meltzer, H. Y., & Lowy, M. T. (1991). The neuroendocrine system and suicide. In L. Davidson & M. Linnoila (Eds.), *Risk factors for youth suicide* (pp. 219–230). New York: Hemisphere.

Moore, P. S. (1986). *Useful information on suicide.* [DHHS Publication No. (ADM) 86–1489]. Rockville, MD: National Institute of Mental Health.

Muse, N. J. (1990). *Depression and suicide in children and adolescents.* Austin, TX: Pro-Ed.

National Center for Health Statistics. (1989). Advance report of final mortality statistics, 1987. [*Monthly Vital Statistics Report, Vol. 38,* No. 5, SupplementaryDHHS Publication]. Hyattsville, MD: U. S. Public Health Service.

Peck, M. L. (1985). Crisis intervention treatment with chronically and acutely suicidal adolescents. In M. L. Peck, N. L. Farberow, & R. E. Litman (Eds.), *Youth suicide (pp. 112–122).* New York: Springer.

Peterson, K. S. (1991, April 2). Suicide by older teens on upswing. *USA Today,* p.1.

Pfeffer, C. R. (1986). *The suicidal child.* New York: The Guilford Press.

Pfeffer, C. R. (1989). Studies of suicidal preadolescent and adolescent inpatients: A critique of research methods. *Suicide and Life-Threatenting Behavior, 19*(1), 58–77.

Pfeffer, C. R., Conte, H. R., Plutchik, R., & Jerrett, I. (1979). Suicidal behavior in latency-age children: An empirical study. *Journal of the American Academy of Child Psychiatry, 18,* 679–692.

Pfeffer, C. R., & Plutchik, R. (1982). Psychopathology of latency-age children: Relation to treatment planning. *Journal of Nervous and Mental Disease, 17,* 193–197.

Pfeffer, C. R., Plutchik, R., Mizruchi, M. S., & Lipkins, R. (1985). *Suicidal behavior in child psychiatric inpatients, outpatients, and nonpatients.* Paper presented at the Annual Meeting of the American Psychiatric Association, Dallas.

Pfeffer, C. R., Solomon, G., Plutchik, R., Mizruchi, M. S., & Weiner, A. (1982). Suicidal behavior in latency-age psychiatric patients: A replication and cross-validation. *Journal of the American Academy of Child Psychiatry, 21,* 564–569.

Pfeffer, C. R., Zuckerman, S., Plutchik, R., & Mizruchi, M. S. (1984). Suicidal behavior in normal school children: A comparison with child psychiatric patients. *Journal of the American Academy of Child Psychiatry, 23*(4), 416–423.

Phillips, D. P. (1974). The influence of suggestion on suicide: Substantive and theoretical implications of the Werther effect. *American Sociological Review, 39,* 340–354.

Phillips, D. P. (1979). Suicide, motor fatalities, and the mass media: Evidence toward a theory of suggestion. *American Journal of Sociology, 84,* 1150–1174.

Phillips, D., & Carstensen, L. (1986). Clustering of teenage suicides after television news stories about suicide. *New England Journal of Medicine, 315,* 685–689.

Phillips, D., & Paight, D. J. (1987). The impact of television movies about suicide: A replicative study. *New England Journal of Medicine, 317,* 809–811.

Poland, S. (1989). *Suicide intervention in the schools.* New York: Guilford.

Puig-Antich, J. (1982). Major depression and conduct disorder in prepuberty. *Journal of the American Academy of Child Psychiatry, 21,* 118–128.

Puig-Antich, J., Blau, S., Marx, N., Greenhill, L. L., & Chambers, W. (1978). Prepubertal major depressive disorder: A pilot study. *Journal of the American Academy of Child Psychiatry, 17,* 695–707.

Puig-Antich, J., & Gittelman, R. (1982). Depression in childhood and adolescence. In E. S. Paykel (Ed.), *Handbook of affective disorders* (pp. 379–392). Edinburgh: Churchill & Livingstone.

Puig-Antich, J., Lukens, E., Davies, M., Goetz, D., Brennan-Quattrock, J., & Todak, G. (1985). Psychosocial functioning in prepubertal major depressive disorders. I. Interpersonal relationships during the depressive episode. *Archives of General Psychiatry, 42,* 500–507.

Robbins, D. R.,& Alessi, N. E. (1985). Depressive symptoms and suicidal behavior in adolescents. *American Journal of Psychiatry, 142,* 588–592.

Rosenthal, P. A., & Rosenthal, S. (1984). Suicidal behavior by preschool children. *American Journal of Psychiatry, 141,* 520–525.

Rutter, M. (1986). The developmental psychopathology of depression: Issues and perspectives. In M. Rutter, C. E. Izard, & P. B. Read (Eds.), *Depression in young people: Developmental and clinical perspectives.* New York: Guilford.

Rutter, M., Tizard, J., & Whitmore, K. (1981). *Education, health, and behavior.* Huntington, NY: Krieger.

Shaffer, D. (1988, April). *School research issues.* Paper presented at the 21st Annual Conference of the American Association of Suicidology. Washington, DC.

Shaffer, D., Garland, A., Gould, M., Fisher, P., & Trautman, P. (1988). Preventing teenage suicide. *Journal of the American Academy of Child and Adolescent Psychiatry, 27*, 675–687.

Shaffer, D., Vieland, V., Garland, A., Rojas, M., Underwood, M., & Busner, C. (1990). Adolescent suicide attempters: Response to suicide-prevention programs. *Journal of the American Medical Association, 264*, 3151–3155.

Slenkovich, J. (1986, June). School districts can be sued for inadequate suicide prevention programs. *The Schools' Advocate*, pp. 1–3.

Smith, K., Eyman, J., Dyck, R., & Ryerson, D. (1987). *Report of a survey of school-related suicide programs*. Committee report to the American Association of Suicidology.

Stanley, M. (1991). Post mortem studies of suicide. In L. Davidson & M. Linnoila (Eds.), *Risk factors for youth suicide* (pp. 197–218). New York: Hemisphere.

Stark, K. (1990). *Childhood depression: School-based intervention*. New York: Guilford.

Trad, P. V. (1986). *Infant depression: Paradigms and paradoxes*. New York: Springer-Verlag.

Weinberg, W., & Rehmet, A. (1983). Childhood affective disorder and school problems. In D. P. Cantwell & G. A. Carlson (Eds.), *Affective disorders in childhood and adolescence: An update* (pp. 109–128). Lancaster, England: MTP Press.

Weinberg, W. A., Rutman, J., Sullivan, L., Penick, E. C., & Dietz, S. G. (1973). Depression in children referred to an educational diagnostic center: Diagnosis and treatment. Preliminary report. *Journal of Pediatrics, 83*, 1065–1072.

Yufit, R. I. (1991). American Association of Suicidology presidential address: Suicide assessment in the 1990s. *Suicide and Life-Threatening Behavior, 21*(2), 152–163.

Zahn-Waxler, C., Mayfield, A., Radke-Yarrow, M., McKnew, D., Cytryn, L., & Davenport, U. (1988). A follow-up investigation of offspring of parents with bipolar disorder. *American Journal of Psychiatry, 145*, 506–509.

Resources

Recent Publications

Blumenthal, S. J., & Kupfer, D. J. (Eds.). (1990). *Suicide over the life cycle: Risk factors, assessment, and treatment of suicidal patients.* Washington, DC: American Psychiatric Association.

Guetzloe, E. C. (1989). *Suicide and depression, the adolescent epidemic: Education's responsibility (rev. ed.).* [Available from Advantage Consultants, Inc., 2016 E. Robinson St., Orlando, FL 32803]. $4.00.

Guetzloe, E. C. (1989). *Youth suicide: What the educator should know.* [Available from The Council for Exceptional Children, 1920 Association Drive, Reston, VA 22091-1589]. $18.50.

Kauffman, J. M. (1989). *Characteristics of behavior disorders of children and youth* (4th ed.). Columbus, OH: Merrill Publishing Company.

Matson, J. L. (1989). *Treating depression in children and adolescents.* New York: Pergamon Press, Inc.

McKnew, D. H., Cytryn, L. & Yahraes, H. (1983). *Why isn't Johnny crying? Coping with depression in children.* New York: W. W. Norton & Company.

Muse, N. J. (1990). *Depression and suicide in children and adolescents.* Austin, TX: Pro-Ed.

Newslink. Quarterly newsletter. [Available from the American Association of Suicidology, 2459 S. Ash, Denver, CO 80222, (303) 692-0985].

Pfeffer, C. R. (1986). *The suicidal child.* New York: The Guilford Press.

Phi Delta Kappa Task Force on Adolescent Suicide. (1988). *Responding to adolescent suicide.* [Available from the Phi Delta Kappa Educational Foundation, P. O. Box 789, Bloomington IN 47402-0789]. $2.00.

Poland, S. (1989). *Suicide intervention in the schools.* New York: The Guilford Press.

Rutter, M., Izard, C. E., & Read, P. B. (Eds.). (1986). *Depression in young people.* New York: The Guilford Press.

Stark, K. (1990). *Childhood depression: School-based intervention.* New York: The Guilford Press.

Suicide and Life-Threatening Behavior. Quarterly journal. [Available from the American Association of Suicidology, 2459 S. Ash, Denver, CO 80222, (303) 692-0985].

Professional Associations and Support Groups

American Academy of Child and Adolescent Psychiatry
3615 Wisconsin Avenue N. W.
Washington, DC 20016
(202) 966-7300

American Association of Suicidology
2459 South Ash
Denver, CO 80222
(303) 692-0985

American Orthopsychiatric Association
19 West 44th Street
Suite 1616
New York, NY 10036

American Psychological Association
1200 17th Street N. W.
Washington, DC 20016
(202) 955-7660

Compassionate Friends, Inc.
P. O. Box 3696
Oak Brook, IL 60521
(312) 323-5010

Council for Children with Behavioral Disorders
A Division of The Council for Exceptional Children
1920 Association Drive
Reston, VA 22091-1589
(703) 620-3660

The Council for Exceptional Children
1920 Association Drive
Reston, VA 22091-1589
(703) 620-3660

National Alliance for the Mentally Ill
1901 North Fort Myer Drive, Suite 500
Arlington, VA 22209-1604
(703) 524-7600

National Depressive and Manic Depressive Association
Merchandise Mart, Box 3395
Chicago, IL 60654
(312) 993-0066

The Samaritans, Inc.
500 Commonwealth Avenue
Boston, MA 02215

Survivors of Suicide
184 Salem Avenue
Dayton, OH 45406
(513) 223-9096

Public and Private Research Centers

Center for Cognitive Therapy
Room 602
133 South 36th Street
Philadelphia, PA 19104

Center for Suicide Research and Prevention
Rush-Presbyterian-St. Luke's Medical Center
1720 West Polk Street
Chicago, IL 60612

Centers for Disease Control
Intentional Injuries Section
Division of Injury Epidemiology and Control
1600 Clifton Road N. E.
Atlanta, GA 30333

National Center on Institutions and Alternatives
(Information on Jail Suicide Prevention)
40 Lantern Lane
Mansfield, MA 02048
(508) 337-8806

National Institute of Corrections (NIC) Information Center
1790 30th Street
Suite 130
Boulder, CO 80301
(303) 939-8877

National Institute of Mental Health
5600 Fishers Lane
Rockville, MD 20857
(301) 443-2403

Office of the Inspector General
U. S. Department of Health and Human Services
2901 Third Avenue, MS 309
Seattle, WA 98121
(206) 442-0491

Suicide Information and Education Centre
201-1615 10th Avenue S.W.
Calgary, Alberta, Canada T3C OJ7
(403) 245-3900

CEC Mini-Library
Exceptional Children at Risk

A set of 11 books that provide practical strategies and interventions for children at risk.

- *Programming for Aggressive and Violent Students.* Richard L. Simpson, Brenda Smith Miles, Brenda L. Walker, Christina K. Ormsbee, & Joyce Anderson Downing. No. P350. 1991. 42 pages.

- *Abuse and Neglect of Exceptional Children.* Cynthia L. Warger with Stephanna Tewey & Marjorie Megivern. No. P351. 1991. 44 pages.

- *Special Health Care in the School.* Terry Heintz Caldwell, Barbara Sirvis, Ann Witt Todaro, & Debbie S. Accouloumre. No. P352. 1991. 56 pages.

- *Homeless and in Need of Special Education.* L. Juane Heflin & Kathryn Rudy. No. P353. 1991. 46 pages.

- *Hidden Youth: Dropouts from Special Education.* Donald L. Macmillan. No. P354. 1991. 37 pages.

- *Born Substance Exposed, Educationally Vulnerable.* Lisbeth J. Vincent, Marie Kanne Poulsen, Carol K. Cole, Geneva Woodruff, & Dan R. Griffith. No. P355. 1991. 28 pages.

- *Depression and Suicide: Special Education Students at Risk.* Eleanor C. Guetzloe. No. P356. 1991. 45 pages.

- *Language Minority Students with Disabilities.* Leonard M. Baca & Estella Almanza. No P357. 1991. 56 pages.

- *Alcohol and Other Drugs: Use, Abuse, and Disabilities.* Peter E. Leone. No. P358. 1991. 33 pages.

- *Rural, Exceptional, At Risk.* Doris Helge. No. P359. 1991. 48 pages.

- *Double Jeopardy: Pregnant and Parenting Youth in Special Education.* Lynne Muccigrosso, Marylou Scavarda, Ronda Simpson-Brown, & Barbara E. Thalacker. No. P360. 1991. 44 pages.

Save 10% by ordering the entire library, No. P361, 1991. Call for the most current price information, 703/620-3660.

Send orders to:
The Council for Exceptional Children, Dept. K11150
1920 Association Drive, Reston VA 22091-1589